THOUGHTS OF YOUR MIND

THOUGHTS OF YOUR MIND

Priya Dabas

KALPAZ

Thoughts of Your Mind

ISBN : 978-81-7835-967-0

Published in 2013 in India by
Kalpaz Publications
C-30, Satyawati Nagar,
Delhi - 110052
E-mail: kalpaz@hotmail.com

Laser Type Setting : Rajender Vashist, Delhi
Printed at : Chawla Offset Printers, Delhi

Foreword

Destinies are based on thought process of human being; and thoughts are based on grooming by parents, teachers, peer groups and legacies of great wisdom ensshrined in the books, sculptures and historical monuments. Even nature has a great impact on the thought process of human soul.

Priya Dabas has made sincere efforts in the collection of great6 thoughts given by various philosophers, from time to time across the globe. I am confident that this collection of wisdom will transform the thought process of readers.

I wish Priya Dabas all the success in fulfilling her mission of changing the thought process of people across all generations.

P.C. JAIN

PRINCIPAL

SRCC

" There is a difference between

interest and commitment

when

You are interested in doing something

You do it only when Circumstances Permit

if

You are committed towards something,

You accept no excuse, only Result "

Learn from the Past

Act in Present

Focus on the task in Hand

Not on the Result...

Take decision at the right Time

rather than the right Decision...

If you want to be at Top

Accept the challenges and be confident

Never give up.

Whenever you fail, Don't forget

There is no Gain without Pain.

Making Mistakes is fine until

you Learn from them.

Anonymous

Keep your face to the Sunshine
and you can not see the Shadows.

We change the world not by what we say or do, but as a consequence of what we have become.

It feels Good to stand on

Ground and watch up High

at your aim

But

It feels Best when you stand up

high and others watch you as

their Aim.

To handle yourself, use your Head

To handle others, use your Heart.

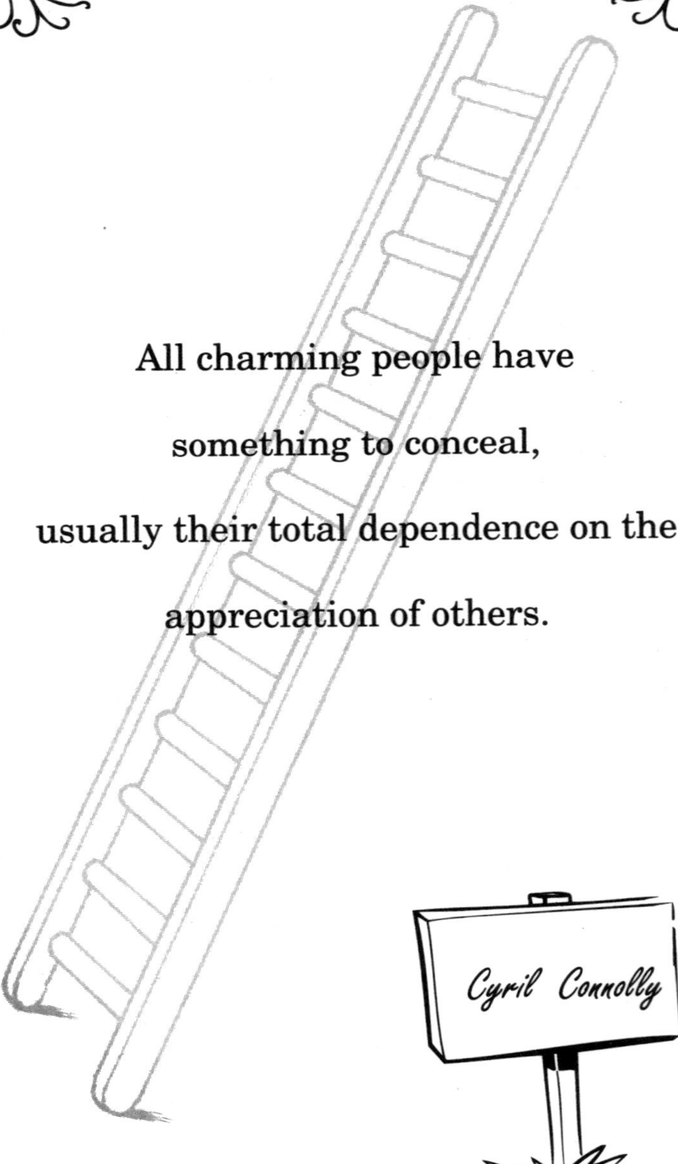

All charming people have

something to conceal,

usually their total dependence on the

appreciation of others.

If you can't change your Fate

change your Attitude.

Courage is what it takes

to stand up and Speak.

Courage is also what it

takes to sit down and Listen.

Reputation is what

Men and Women

think of us.

Character is what God

and

Angels know of us.

In Prosperity our friends

know us,

In Adversity we know our friends.

A Strong positive mental

Attitude creats more

Miracles than any wonder drug.

Slow down and enjoy Life

It's not only the scenery

you miss by going fast,

you also Miss the sense of where

you are Going and Why.

Eddie Cantor

Past is to Learn

Present is to Perform

and

Future to Plan

Time changes everything except something within us which is always Surprised by Change.

Efforts may fail, but don't fail

to make Efforts.

I am only one

But still I am one

I cannot do Everything.

But still I can do Something

And because I cannot do Everything

I will not refuse to do the Something

That I can Do !

Your mind is a Garden

your thoughts are the Seeds

the harvest can be either Flowers or Weeds.

Smile more

Don't take life too Seriously

see the Funny side of whatever happens.

Life is 10 per cent what

Happens to you and

90 per cent how you

Respond to it.

More people spend more time

and energy going around Problems

Than in trying to Solve them.

Some men have thousand reasons why they cannot do what they want to, when all they need is one reason why they Can.

Knowing what you cannot Do

is more Important than

knowing what you can do

In fact, that's good Taste.

Lucille Ball

Luck is quite Predictable

If you want more luck, take more chances

Be more Active...

Winning horse in a Race

Does not know why it Runs in Race,

It runs because of the beating and Pains,

...The Larger you get Pain,

The Stronger you become,

Life is a race

God is our rider,

So if u r in pain than think

God wants you to Win the race.

Anonymous

I like the dreams of the Future better than the History of the Past.

You can't change

your Destination overnight

but you can change your Direction overnight.

Believe in yourself ! have faith

in your Abilities

without a humble but reasonable

confidence in your own Powers

you cannot be Successful or Happy.

Time is too Slow for those

who wait...

too Swift for those

who fear...

too Long for those

who grieve...

too Short for those

who rejoice...

but for those

who love, time is Eternity...

Success is a Journey,

not a Destination.

Success is the progressive

Achievement of

worthy and challenging

Goals or Dreams.

There are two kinds of people

on the road of life

PASSENGERS and DRIVERS

Now you have to decide

what you want to be...

Success is getting

what you Want.

Happiness is wanting,

what you Get.

A very small degree of Hope

is sufficient to make the birth of Love.

Stendhal

They are ill Discovers that

think there is no land

when,

you can see nothing but sea.

General knowledge are those knowledge which idiots possess, to particularize is alone the distinction of Merit.

Don't take Excuse

instead

take Efforts.

What ever you have

you are responsible for it.

If you are looking for big opportunity

you find big Difficulty.

I believe in the dignity of Labour,

whether with head or hand,

that the world owes every man

an Opportunity to make a living.

Be strong ! The sign of Life is

strength and growth.

The sign of Death is weakness

whatever is weak, avoid!

It is death ....

If you want be have Life

You have to Die

every moment for it.

Love is like dew that falls

on both nettles and lilies.

With Courage you will

dare to take Risks

Courage is the foundation of Integrity.

Take nothing but Pictures
leave nothing but Footprints
kill nothing but Time.
B.G. Motto

No human condition

is ever Permanent

So you should not be overjoyed

in Good Fortune nor too scornful

in Misfortune.

Write injuries in Dust

but kindness in Marble.

There is nothing either

Good or Bad but

thinking makes it so.

The roots of education are

Bitter but the fruit is Sweet.

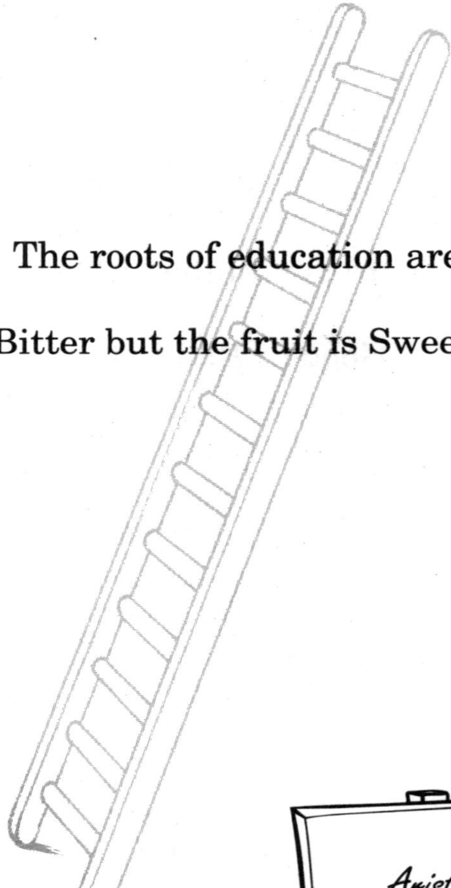

The first step to getting the things

you want out of life is -

'Decide what you Want'...

Ben Stein

People are just Happy as

they make up their Minds to be.

The real friend is one
who Walks in when the rest
of world Walks out.

If you walk "you defenetly find the way "

It's not how much or how Little you

have that makes you great or small

But how much or how Little you are with

what you have.

All of us do not have
Equal Talent but all of
us should have an Equal
Opportunity to develop our talents.

John F Kennedy

Destiny is no matter of Chance

It is a matter of Choice

It is not a thing to be waited for

It is a thing to be Achieved.

What ever you do

Devote your Heart, Mind and

Soul to it.

If you fail,

you suicide.

You again fail,

In the battle of life.

Confidence ! like an art, never

comes with having all the answers,

It comes from being

open to the questions.

Aim is not for what you are

but what you could be

Challenge yourself

and

Release your hidden Potential.

Don't cry because it's over.

Smile because it happened.

There are two ways

of meeting Difficulties

you alter the Difficulties

or you alter yourself to meet them.

Remember the two Benefits of failure

First,

If you do fail, you learn what doesn't work

and second,

The failure gives you the opportunity to

try with a new Approach.

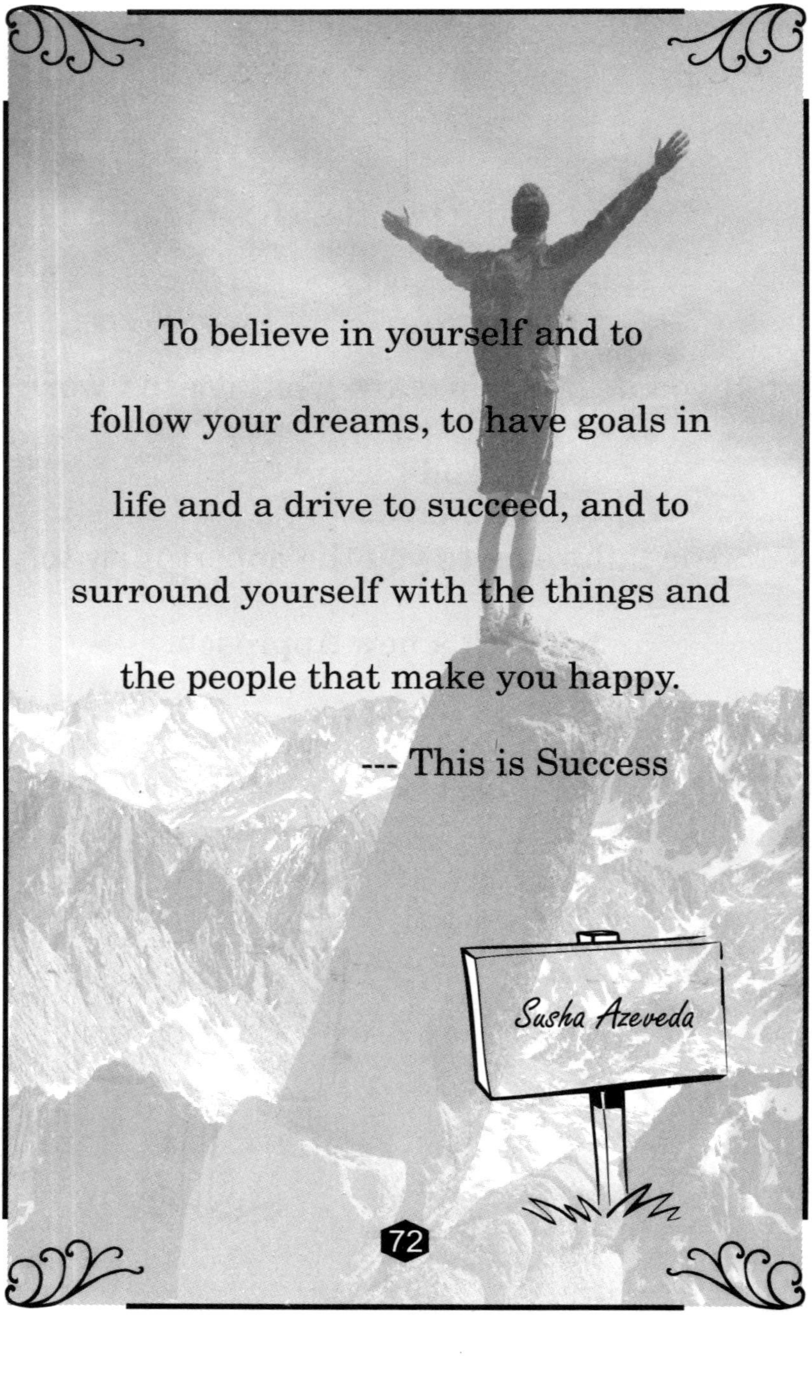
To believe in yourself and to follow your dreams, to have goals in life and a drive to succeed, and to surround yourself with the things and the people that make you happy.
--- This is Success
Susha Azeveda

The more you praise

and celebrate your life the more there is in

life to celebrate.

There are only two way to live Life

One is as though nothing is a miracle

The other is as though

everything is a Miracle.

One who ask a question is

a fool for five Minutes

but one who does not ask a question

remains a fool Forever.

It takes a little courage and

a little self control

and some grim determination

no mater what the battle

if you are really out to Win.

When you come to the end

of your Rope, tie a knot & hang on.

As a single foot step will not make

a path on the earth,

so a single thought will not

make a pathway in the mind.

Anonymous